How To Coach
BATTING

Dr. A.K. Srivastava

M.P.Ed., N.I.S. (Athletics), D.Y. Ed., Ph.D. (Phy. Edu.)
Director, Physical Education
Delhi Engineering College, Bawana Road, Delhi-110042

SPORTS PUBLICATION

7/26, Ground Floor, Ansari Road, Darya Ganj,
New Delhi-110 002. Ph.: (O) 55749511, 55257538
(M) 9868028838 (R) 27562163

Published by:

SPORTS PUBLICATION
H.O.: 7/26, Ground Floor, Ansari Road,
Darya Ganj, New Delhi-110 002.
Ph. : (O) 55749511, 55257538 (R) 27562163, (M) 9868028838
E-mail: *ektathani@hotmail.com/ lakshaythani@hotmail.com*
Website : www.sportspublication.trade-india.com

I.S.B.N. – 81-7879-231-1

PRINTED IN INDIA 2006

Laser Typeset by:
JAIN MEDIA GRAPHICS, Delhi-110035. Ph.: 27190244

Printed by:
CHAWLA OFFSET PRINTERS, Delhi-110052

Price: Rs. 140/-

PREFACE

How to Coach Batting is yet another voyage in the field of sports and physical education. By going through this book, any aspirant learner may definitely understand and sharp his batting skills which is integral part of the game of cricket. It includes all the essentials ingredients of batting viz., skills, techniques, latest rules and court measurements and dimensions along with relevant illustrations.

The texts are critically arranged in a such a manner that a learner feels ease while reading the texts and learning the skills, tactics, strategies, rules etc. of Batting. The language used while composing the texts are basically simple colloquial English. The present study has a wide scope for everyone who wish to gain their knowledge towards this great game. Historical background, Skills, tactics, and techniques, latest amended rules with court dimensions and measurements are explained in lucid form and in a simple English keeping in mind the language difficulty of the students of physical education.

Hopefully, the present study will prove very handy and useful for the those involved in the field of physical education and sports specially cricket, prospective coaches, aspirant cricketer wish to sharp his batting skills, sports personalities, teachers, students of physical education, children as well as for the general readers. Thus, the present study has a-z of batting which a cricketer, learner, aspirant player is looking for.

— **Dr. A.K. Srivastava**

CONTENTS

1

INTRODUCTION

45, sikh

Batting is the backbone of cricket sport. Oftenly, great young cricketers used to catch the glimpses of the spectators. Batting is one of the important ingredients of cricket and therefore it should be tackled seriously. Batting skills demands appropriate timings and judgement while playing the ball.

Very oftenly, some aspirants used to be naturally outfit for cricket such as Sachin Tendulkar, Late Don Bradman etc. The greatest of players can improve by means of concentration and practices but the natural athlete must start with a great advantage. One hall-mark of good batting is that the player appears to have plenty of time in which to play his shots.

Some players are marvellous at the nets but cannot reproduce their form in matches. Others are poor net players but succeed because they possess the so-called "big match temperament". A tremendous premium must be placed on this peculiar characteristic, which is probably more essential for a batsman than any form of sport some people can think so.

The golfer may fluff his drive, the tennis player miss his smash and so on, there is still time to recover, but one mistake by a batsman and there is no second chance. Hand in hand with temperament must go concentration, which can and must be cultivated by anyone who wishes to rise to international standards. It is one of the essentials. Moreover, the concentration needs to be harnessed for long periods.

Many batsmen can survive a short period figures, but they are unable to keep going. Test cricket demands the utmost concentration for hours on end.

There are two following methods of playing which a ideal batsmen should follow:

(a) concentrate and (b) watch the ball.

They could well be the last words before anyone goes in to bat. Watching the ball means that the batsman must first carefully observe the bowler's hand as he is in the act of delivering the ball.

The movement of hand and arm gives the first clue as to the bowler's intentions—whether he is trying to impart off spin, leg spin or something else. Once the ball leaves the hand, the ball must be the sole object of your attention. Undoubtedly some people have keener eyesight than others.

The wizard Ranjitsinghji was supposed to see the ball very clearly. Indeed, there is a story that a certain prominent batsman on being questioned as to his own ability to see the ball said, "Yes, I had good eyesight—I could see the seams, but Ranjit could see the stitches." In his early years a batsman should be able to see the ball turning in the air as it comes down the pitch towards him when the bowler is a slow spinner. This is necessary against a today's class googly bowlers like Muttahaiya Muralitharan of Sri Lanka, Shane Warne of World Champion Team Australia and Anil Kumble of India.

Even if the bowler disguises his googly you still have the added insurance of watching the spin of the ball to make sure which way it will turn on pitching. Try to glue the eyes on the ball until the very moment it hits the bat. This cannot always be achieved in practice but try. Blessed is the boy who finds himself possessed of these attributes as a natural gift. But like the boy prodigy who, at, say, five years of age, finds himself able to play the piano, practice and more practice is needed to perfect his talent. The fellow who sees the ball leave the bowler's hand, see it land and then plays "at the pitch", is always in trouble when the ball moves in the air of after hitting the ground. It is advisable to all the aspirant new players who is interested in batting to play with a ball at every opportunity.

Whether it be a golf ball, tennis ball, baseball or any other kind doesn't matter. It will help the learner to train the eye and co-ordinate brain, eye and muscle. When it comes to detailed execution of that art, batting at the nets is the first method of improving one's efficiency.

So many things can be tried out there. You can perform experiment with your grip, your stance, stroke execution, etc., until satisfied you have the right method. Throughout his career a batsman, even though he may have achieved fame, must continue assiduously at net practice.

A player who was to bat that day, and upon whom a heavy responsibility lay, was observed incivilian clothes on the balcony outside the players dressing-room five minutes before play was due to commence. He was in full view of the public and the opposing team. He failed miserably—a just reward. Confidence in one's own ability is admirable in moderation but it does not absolve anyone from the need for practice. The early formative years of a boy's career can have a tremendous bearing on his technique. Mostly world class crickerts like Don Bradman, Kapil Dev etc., learnt their cricket on hard wickets and undoubtedly this was responsible for the development of certain shots in preference to others.

But it does not in any sense alter the cardinal virtues, such as "watching the ball", which are common under all conditions. Take full advantage of your natural assets, improve them and adapt them to changing circumstances. It is a good idea to try to obtain net practice against the type of bowler who worries you most, or against whom you expect to play in forthcoming matches.

An outstanding example of this need was the 1956 tour of England by Australia. To the most casual observer it was obvious that the Australians were having more trouble with off-spinner Laker than any other type. It was a clear case where net practice against off-spinners was a cardinal need. Whilst it is true that some players are born, or achieve greatness without coaching, and equally true that some players are overcoached.

2

BATTING—
BRIEF HISTORY

Cricket was firstly came into sight in England. Cricket has developed from a crude game which was played as early as the 12th century; but the first real cricket club to be established was the Hambledon Club, which flourished in the second half of the 18th century. This was followed, in 1787, by the Marylebone Cricket Club, which later made its headquarters at Lords's in St. John's Wood, London; and since that day the M.C.C. has been the recognized authority on all cricket affairs. Cricket was originally played on ordinary English meadow-land, with long uncut grass for the outfield, and only the actual pitch was scythed.

Later, light wooden rollers were used on the wicket, sheep were used to keep the grass down to a reasonable height and a 'boundary line' was marked all round the field. These improvements made for much higher scoring, because not only did the ball run over the ground much easier but also the batsmen did not become so tired when it became no longer necessary to run out 'boundaries'. The next step was the inclusion of a rule which allowed the actual pitch to be brushed, swept and rolled after each innings.

Later still, the hand mower made another big improvement, first to the state of the wicket and then to the whole outfield. The scoring was originally performed by a 'notcher', who cut a notch in a stick whenever a run was scored. Village cricket in Kent and Sussex was probably the first true home of the game, which steadily grew and developed, in spite of a rather dark period when a considerable amount of gambling and wagering on results took place.

A great deal of the history of cricket may be learned from a visit to the pavilion of the preset Lord's Cricket Ground. Thomas Lord was the original owner of the ground; he took it over in 1814 after he had owned previous cricket grounds in Dorset Square and North Bank, and it has been known as Lord's ever since.

Amongst the many interesting paintings in the Long Room is one of Lord's in 1837, showing the M.C.C. Jubilee match—North versus South—in progress. If we look at it very carefully, we can see a pleasant little pavilion, rather like a modern school cricket pavilion, a big flagstaff with an enormous flag flying, spectators sitting on benches—one onlooker at deep mid-on is actually seated on a horse.

In the early days, it must be remembered, all bowling was underhand, but in 1825 round arm bowling was permitted. This meant that the ball could be delivered at any angle so long as the and was not above the elbow. The chief consequence of this was that bowling became faster but less accurate, and many balls were so erratic that they beat both the wicket-keeper and his assistant, the long-stop. The actual origin of over-arm bowling is uncertain, although a certain John Willes of Sutton Valence is often given the credit for discovering it.

It is said that he got the idea from his sister when she bowled or probably threw at him in practice. Orthodox bowling at the time was still underhand, and when, in one important match at Lord's, Wiles was no-balled for his new action, the story goes that he flew into such a temper that he jumped on his horse, rode out of the ground and never played cricket again. It is a far cry from those primitive days to our highly organized modern cricket matches.

In this way, cricket batting which emerged from the primitive days flourished and developed as the important and backbone of cricket.

3

THE GRIP

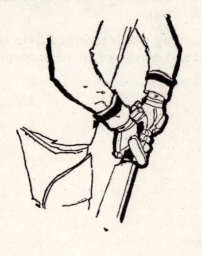

Both the right-handed batsman and left-handed batsman have to follow the same principles of batting grip.

The right-handed batsman should hold the bat in a position that his left hand should hold the top of the handle. While in case cf a left-handed batsman, the top of the handle should be hold with right hand.

While holding the bat while batting, the batsman should follow the following coaching tips carefully:

Coaching Tip 1

1. The batsman should hold the bat from the top of the handle with both hands.

2. The batsman should hold the bat in a position that 'V' shape is formed by thumb and forefinger point.

Coaching Tip 2

1. The batsman should hold the bat in a position that his top hand rests comfortably on the inside of the front thigh. This will becomes opposite in case the batsman is right hander.

2. The batsman should stand in a position that the back of the top hand should face towards extra cover.

THE IDEAL GRIP

The ideal grip for the batsman is to hold the bat handle with the hands close together not too tight and not too loose. The batsman should hold the bat close together with both hands in the centre of the bat handle. The batsman should hold the bat in a position that his thumb and forefinger should create 'v' shape. The batsman should always hold the bat not too tightly and not too loose; the bat should be in a position to play the variety of batting strokes.

The bat grip is the first step towards batsmanship, obviously very important. A correct grip gives your batting the full flair and does not restrict your range of shots. The ideal grip prescribed above is a distinct advantage to have as a batsman, but do not make the mistake of forcing yourself into the correct grip.

Try it for a few days see how it goes .Discard it if you do not quite find it comfortable. Thats the key, comfort. You have to be comfortable with your grip. Some cricket experts has rightly said, "Its got to feel right. Its good to have the ideal grip but it does not guarantee success." Great batsmen are proof of that. All of them did not have the ideal grip.

Its always a good idea to keep the top hand tighter on the bat handle.

4

THE STANCE

THE IDEAL STANCE

The batsman should stand properly with his feets comfortably apart. The batsman should stand neither close nor too wide besides the crease.

While tackling the balls from the bowler, the batsman should keep his body weight on the feet and not on the heels. The body weight should be equally divided on both feets. The batsman's front shoulder should point straight down the pitch in line with the stumps at the opposite end, that is always a good indicator.

While tackling the ball, the batsman's knees slightly bent. The batsman should stand firmly and still. The eyes of the batsman should be steady and firm and should watch the ball all the time. The batsman's bat should be grounded just around the toes of his back foot.

STANCE MADE SIMPLE

A good stance is a well balanced stance! You may not fulfill all the requirements of the ideal stance mentioned above but if you feel nicely balanced and relaxed in your position to face the ball, you are in a better position to judge the ball and play your desired strokes in the field.

Very oftenly, before the ball is delivered many young batsman commit the mistake of lifting the bat straight in stance. This is in an effort to keep the bat straight but this will unbalance you. The batsman should allow himself to lift the bat in stance, from the direction of third slip or gully as the bowler runs in . It helps greatly in the balance. But remember, when the bat comes down to meet the ball it must come down as straight as possible. This is vitally important to survive at the highest level.

So remember good balance, Bat feeling a part of yourself ,weight on the balls of the feet so you are quick to react. These are the things you concentrate on with your stance.

The main purposes of the initial position when awaiting delivery of the ball is to be in such a comfortably relaxed and well-balanced position that you are able to go forward or back, attack or defend, with equal speed. The knees should be slightly relaxed.

It is a mistake to rough right over or to stand completely erect. Quite a large number of players stand with their feet together. Most ideal batsmen do not prefer this position because it militates against balance and speed of movement and, infact, necessitates a preliminary change of foot position to obtain proper balance before one can move into a stroke. The rear foot should be at least a couple of inches behind the batting crease.

This is to allow for a slight drag when playing forward. Remember the foot must be behind the crease to avoid a stumping. On the line is out. The front foot should be parallel to the batting crease and some three inches in front of it. Should the front toe be turned slightly towards cover that would not be wrong. Looking down the pitch from the bowler's end, the batsman's toes should be just about in line with the let stump.

Great batsmen like Sachin Tendulkar, Sanath Jayasurya, Ricky Ponting, Adam Gilchrist etc., usually allow their bat to rest on the ground between their feet simply because it was a comfortable and natural position. Moreover, it will help them to play freely their desired strokes in the area they wish to play.

The position encourages a straighter back lift, is perhaps sounder for defensive play, but it has great limitations in versatile stroke making. There is a possibility that the batting glove may get caught in the top of the pad. For this reason ideal batsmen always lifted their wrists and patted the pitch at least once in taking up their stance to ensure the hands were completely free. Cricket, too, possesses its "waggles" or mannerisms. But before the ball was delivered he would pat the ground with his bat and return to an evenly balanced position. The left shoulder should be pointing down the pitch or very nearly so, with the head turned so that both eyes are clearly focused on the bowler.

One often hears about the two-eyed stance. This is a misnomer. What people really mean is a stance where the shoulders bowler. A chesty stance is wrong because it prevents the batsman getting into the correct driving position. But obviously nobody would be silly enough to try to watch the bowler with one eye only.

It is extremely significant to keep the head as still as possible during one's movement into a shot. That may sound absurd, for obviously the head must move if he body does.

There should be no bobbing or weaving about and that nay jerky movement which might cause a batsman to take his eye off the flight of the ball is dangerous. The batsman should concentrate his eyes on the ball and it is surprising how natural the body movement becomes. Once again comfort and relaxation are the key words.

5

FRONT FOOT DEFENCE

The ideal front foot defence usually played by the ideal batsman to a ball pitched on the good length.

This type of defensive stroke should be used when the ball is pitched farther up than a good length and is on, or very close to, a direct line between the two sets of stumps. Its purpose is to smother any Spain or swing which may be on the ball.

Supposing the ball was spinning so much that it changed course from leg to off five degrees on hitting the ground. If allowed to travel a mere six inches after pitching before hitting the blade, this deviation would not matter. But if allowed to travel a few feet, it might touch the edge of the bat for a catch in the slips.

Obviously, therefore, to play forward to a short, pitched ball is bad theory. It is desirable in forward to keep the bat absolutely perpendicular throughout, therefore a reasonably straight back lift is required. The handle of the bat should be kept forward of the glade in order that the ball will be kept down.

The batsman should always play close to the front leg, this will make the batsman ease while tackling the ball. The batsman should lean forward his shoulder and elbow while tackling the ball. The batsman should bend the left knee slightly to hold the weight of the body in balance and point the left toe towards mid-off or cover, varying it slightly according to the direction of the ball.

If the ball is pitched on the leg stump, for instance, the left toe will point more towards the bowler than it would be for a ball pitched, say, just outside the off stump.

The batsman should keep his head well forward and down. At the end to the stroke the right toe will be the balancing agent at the rear and it must be kept firmly behind the batting crease. This precaution is necessary in case the ball misses the bat and the question of a stumping arises. One of the cricket's simplest errors is for a batsman to misjudge the length of a ball, play forward and be beaten by spin or swing.

The tendency then is to overbalance forward—hence the need for keeping that right toe firmly down. In forward defence the left hind is in control. Note: The right-hand grip should always be changed until it has become almost a thumb and first two fingers only at the bottom of the handle. The right hand acts really as a guide. No power is required.

Taking Guard or Block

Every batsman, upon arriving at the crease, must take block. There are three common positions; middle stump, leg stump, and two legs stump.

It was heard once that a batsman ask for middle and leg inclined to leg, but it is thought that he was stretching things a bat too far. The sole purpose of taking guard is to enable the batsman to judge the direction of the ball relative to his wicket. Spectators sometimes wonder why batsmen may ask for guard several times during an innings. The answer is that a mark on the ground may become obliterated or damaged. Very oftenly, the two batsmen at the wickets possesses the different block or one of them may be a left-handed batsman.

Obviously the one is inclined to make rather a mess of the other fellow's mark, especially if he is the nervous type who is constantly patting the ground whilst awaiting delivery of the ball. The springs can also tear across one's mark when making certain foot movements.

It hardly make any difference on the batsman's play on the basis of his possession of guard, some batsman like to play in the middle and most serviceable areas, while other prefer to play on the backfoot. This meant that the batsman legs are straightened originally some two inches more towards the leg side than they would be if you look middle stump.

In this way it is easier to be sure that a ball travelling towards your pads is outside the leg stumps. And precise judgement of the direction of a ball is a "must" in developing the batting art. When an off-break bowler is operating to a strong leg field, many batsmen take guard on the leg stump or even, in extreme cases, just outside.

By so doing they endeavour to counter his wiles. They

feel it gives them greater freedom to hit at any ball directed at their pads, and a better chance of steering away from the clutching hands of leg slips any ball directed at the stumps. There is much to be said for the theory. On the other hand a batsman whose great weakness is that he fails to cover the ball outside the off-stump especially against a fast or medium-pace attack, would be wise to consider taking middle stump for his guard. It would take him those extra couple of inches towards the line of flight before the ball is delivered. So take your choice. You will have to stand or fall by your judgement.

Usually, some batsmen stretched out front foot to the pitch of the ball while keeping the back foot grounded. This is oftenly seen in Sachin Tendulkar's batting.

The front knee should be slightly bent. The bat should be slightly in front of the leading leg. The palms should be softly placed on the bat. The face of the bat should be straightened facing down the pitch. The head should remain on top of the ball.

The most important thing to do is get as close to the pitch of the ball as possible. Front leg besides the pitch of the ball and not in line of the pitching of the ball. Bending of the front knee is vital helps get on top of the ball better. Position of the head extremely important get it on top of the ball and getting low on the ball is also a good idea. Don't push at the ball once you have decided to defend the ball.

The batsman should keep his arms relaxed not too stiff and strong. Relax your palms. Get the ball dead, close to you. That is good defence. Away from those close catchers.

6

FORWARD DEFENCE

The ball which bounces in line within just outside the line of the stumps is called *The Length ball*. This delivery is termed as a good length ball because it create problems and confusions for the batsman to play the either strokes. The ball bounces just outside the reach of the batsman stepping and stretching forward from his crease.

Backlift

The batsman usually lift the bat at back level in line with the stumps as soon as the bowler prepare to bowl.

Head and shoulder movement

The batsman usually move his head in line with the

ball. The chief feature of this stroke is that the batsman's head and shoulder remain in line of the pitch of the ball.

Foot Movement

The batsman should put the front foot towards and alongside the line of the ball as close as possible to its bounce.

The batsman should transfer his body weight to his front foot in such a manner that his front toe should point to the extra cover and mid-off regions.

Weight transfer and body position

To play forward defence stroke, the batsman should transfer his body position and weight by adhering to the following measures :

1. To play forward defence, the batsman should bent his front knee and should transfer his body weight onto his front foot.

2. The batsman should spread his back leg and grounded on the inside of the toe, thus the batsman is able to transfer correct body weight in order to play forward defence stroke.

3. The batsman should tucked his head into the shoulder. He should slightly bend his left elbow along with the front hip as a unit in a leaning position.

Bat Swing

The batsman should swing down his bat perpendicularly from the top of the backlift along with the top hand controlled and the bottom hand in a position of changing forefinger or thumb grip.

The batsman should end up his bat swing in such a manner that his front leg should not leave any relevant gap between his bat and pad.

The bottom of the bat must remain behind the top of the handle and contact point on the bat is as close as possible in a vertical line with the eyes.

No follow thorough should be made and thus the toe of the bat should not be grounded in any way.

Common Errors

The batsman should taken the following precautions to avoid the common errors occurred while playing this stroke :

1. The batsman should not take his left front foot away from the front foot, thus bending his left knee.

2. The batsman should not make the left hand and arm control stroke.

3. The batsman should always keep his head and shoulder in line with the pitch of the ball all the time, he plays this stroke.

4. The batsman should not place his right toe on the ground while playing forward defence.

5. There should be no such uncertainty in the batsman's mind about the length of the delivery and consequent insurances about whether to play forward or backward.

6. The batsman should not move the full face of his bat along the line of the ball, thus, he fails to play close to the bounce of the ball approaching him.

7. The batsman should not stand and play close enough to the pad.

8. The batsman should play across the line of crease, this will make him comfortable and free to play his desired strokes.

7

BACK FOOT DEFENCE

Back Foot Defence is one of the important strokes of cricket. It is applied by almost all the great and experts batsmen. The batsman should play it by the back foot well back into his stumps in line with the off stump. The front foot follows. The batsman should stay side on. The front elbow should be rises up in line with the ball. The batsman should loose on the handle of the bat while playing back foot defence stroke. The whole body weight should be brought in the front while playing this stroke.

When playing back defensively it is believed that the back lift should be as straight as conveniently possible, and that in its down ward path the bat should pass just outside the right pad as it comes forward to meet the ball. In this shot most batsmen always used more right hand, both in the back lift and the down ward movement, than in the forward defence.

There is an important reason. Suppose your are playing back to an off break pitched a couple of inches outside the off stump, and the ball, after pitching turns across on to the middle and leg stumps. It would no longer be any use playing dead straight towards the pitch of the ball. It would be necessary to follow the direction of the ball, and to do this some power or impetus must come from the right hand which can't therefore be entirely relaxed.

That change of direction to follow the ball cannot satisfactory be controlled by the left hand. Also it is possible to move into position for a back defensive stroke but later convert it into an attacking shot if you see fit to do so. But when purely on the defensive there should be little or no follow through. At least the left hand must be powerful enough to restrict any tendency to follow through too soon, whereby off a rising ball there might be a catch to a close-in fieldsman. Coinciding with the initial movement of taking the bat back, the right foot must be moved back and across in front of the stumps.

The left foot is automatically brought across so that the stumps are completely protected. Advantage should be taken of the areas between the batting crease and the stumps, a distance of four feet.

Obviously one cannot go back the full distance, but even two feet extra in which to sight the ball helps a lot. When in form mostly batsmen like Sanath Jayasurya of Sri Lanka, Virender Sehwag of India etc., liked to feel in playing back defensively that they were hitting the ball either towards cover. It gave them a feeling of security that they were, if anything, coming from outside the line of flight and therefore guarding against a possible slip catch from the ball which went away to the off.

It is so much easier to follow the ball which goes towards the leg side. Some coaches advocate that the toes shall remain parallel with the popping crease— others that they should point towards the bowler. Mostly batsmen favour to play back foot defence by keeping the toes to be pointing rather towards cover or mid-off. Back defensive play is vital.

In order to play accurately this stroke, the batsman should keep his body weight on the right foot, leaving the movement of the left as more of a balancing medium. The right hand slides down to the bottom of the handle to give added control though, as described earlier, the grip is firm. Study the movie strips and the coordinated movement is easily followed.

The batsman should keep his head well over the line of flight and down. Lifting the head is fatal and generally results in cocking the ball up or hitting it on the edge. It is not a bad idea to practice back and forward defence in front of a mirror to see precisely where the batsmen feet are placed and to follow the movement of their bat.

Back Foot Defence Made Easy

This stroke is widely used by almost all the class batsmen in order to tackle the fast bowlers. The batsman should keep his eyes on the ball approaching to him, he should well judge the ball, rock back quickly close to the stumps by making use of sufficient space provided in the batting crease.

While playing back foot defence, the batsman should keep his body weight on his feet and not on the heels. His left elbow should be high with the head in the front. He should not push too much with bottom hand. He should keep his hands softly and closely tucked to his body.

REVIEW OF BACK FOOT DEFENCE STROKE

In order to play back foot defence stroke, the batsman should be taken the following measures :

To what sort of ball:

1. The batsman should not endeavour to play back foot defence to every deliveries. He should go for it only to the short pitch and bouncing balls above waist height.

2. The batsman should swing his bat in line with the pitch of the ball, the bowler bowls.

3. The batsman should move back his head and shoulder directly behind the line of the ball.

4. The batsman should keep his head steady.

5. The eye's level of the batsman should be alongside his leading shoulder.

Foot movement

Back foot moves back and across, just inside the line of the ball parallel with the batting and bowling creases.

Draw front foot back to your back foot with the front foot acting as a balancing agent with its toes slightly resting on the ground.

Body Positioning

The batsman should follow the following tips for keeping his body position while playing back foot defence stroke :

1. He should aim on his front elbow and shoulder at the ball with the hip positioning at mid-on.

2. The batsman should transfer his body weight on the back foot and thus make a complete counter balance to play back foot defence stroke.

3. The batsman should stand on the crease in such a way that his chest should faces the cover point.

4. The batsman should keep his front elbow upwards in vertical direction in order to play the back foot defence stroke.

Coaching Tips

The batsman should follow the following coaching tips in order to play the back foot defence stroke:

1. The batsman should brush the side of his back leg with his bat and should play close to his body.

2. The batsman should make close contact underneath the eyes thus forming a vertical through the contact point and eyes.

3. The batsman should swings down his bat perpendicularly from the top of the backlift with a bent front elbow pointing upwards.

4. The batsman should keep the bottom of his bat must remain behind the handle of the bat with the top in control and the bottom hand changing in a forefinger and thumb grip.

5. The batsman should keep his right elbow tucked in the body in such a manner that his body should not leave any gap between the bat and the body.

6. The batsman should end up his bat swing along his back foot with no follow through.

7. The batsman should keep the bottom of his bat behind the contact point while playing the stroke

Common Errors

The batsman should be very careful and should pay particular attention in order to avoid the following errors and faults in playing the back foot defence stroke :

1. The batsman should not let his top hand control the bat.

2. The batsman should not keep his sideways to the line of the stroke.

3. The batsman should not lift his hands up so high in the back lift.

4. The batsman should not step far enough back with the back foot and not moving far enough to get on the line of the ball.

5. The batsman should not keep his top elbow high enough.

6. The batsman should not keep his head and balance of the body forward while facing the delivery.

8

LATE CUT
OR
BACK CUT

Modern players tend to play the late cut altogether and their expressed reason is "too dangerous". Providing proper judgement is used the rewards to be gained from the shot are well worth the risk. It should only be attempted when the ball is reasonably short of a length and not bouncing very high but is pitched well outside the off stump—it is cut rather in their direction of third or even second slip—and instead of hitting at right angles to the flight as with a square cut, the bat runs in an extreme case almost parallel with the line of flight at contact. The ball is actually hit down on to the ground.

It is normally on the rise when struck and therefore

a snick is almost certain to result in a catch to the wicket-keeper. That is why extreme care and precision are required. It is usually unsafe to try the stroke against fast bowlers. The safety margin is too small and, anyway, fast bowlers usually have slip fieldsmen who would be in the way. Likewise it is very dangerous against off-spinners, but against medium-pace or leg-break bowlers there is a good chance of reward. Power comes mainly from the wrists, but the ball's own momentum is the chief source of its speed.

The stroke is a short, snappy one and not a long swing. After contact with the ball, the end of the bat should go straight down and almost hit the ground. In fact some players do actually hit the ground.

This is a good indication of playing the shot correctly. Whether to risk the stroke or not will be governed by the type of pitch and bowler and the position of the fieldsmen. It may not be worth while for a chance single, but it may well be if a certain four is in the offing.

This shot is divided into two categories, namely Cut off the back and Cut off the front foot. This shot should not be used by beginners on sticky wickets, broken or spinning wickets, very fast wickets. If they try, they are liable to misjudge and mistime the shot. The ideal wicket is of medium pace where the ball comes at an even height. The selection of the ball is an important factor.

The line of the ball should be fixed up to two feet outside the off stump. This shot is made by the horizontal swing of the bat. In the cut off, the back foot, the right foot should be placed in the direction of the gully and according to the distance of the ball from the off stump.

To play the shot, the batsman should transfer his body weight on the right foot. The left shoulder of the batsman should be kept free in order to provide appropriate follow through and make the shot easy to play, in order to get this situation, the batsmen keep his left foot in the same position only his heel should be lifted to provide support to his left shoulder and thus make the late cut more accurate to play. The batsman should keep his elbows straight, his shoulders should be kept parallel to the ground at the time he face the delivery.

If either shoulder gets away from the parallel, a serious defect becomes apparent in the execution of the stroke. The back lift is very important. The arms should not be raised to any degree. At the time of pick-up, the left hand holds the bat firmly and the right hand moves down holding it equally firmly.

Immediately after the impact the right wrist turns over the left so as to keep the ball on the ground. The shot should be practised without a ball to ensure correctness of method. In the variations of the cut, all the foregoing principles are to be observed. If the ball keeps low, the batsman should bend over with his body, not go down by bending his legs.

It is a treat to watch a batsman executing the late cut. It is one of the most difficult shot to execute and the youngster should not try it until he gets control over the other strokes. This shot is made to a ball pitched up to two feet away from the off stump. Under no circumstance, it should be attempted to an incoming ball, meaning an off-break or an in-swinger.

It will invariably take the inner edge of the bat and the result will be disastrous. The right toe points in the direction of the intended stroke and the batsman's back is almost turned on the bowler. The head and body will follow the movement of the right foot. The head will lead the stroke in the direction in which the right foot is pointing, finishing over or even beyond the right foot.

There will be a pronounced bend of the waist for the actual weight and follow-through.

There should be appropriate and proper back lift for the late cut. The forearms and wrists moving round the body will extend the normal back lift upwards and backwards towards the fine-leg so that at the top of the back lift, the back of the bat is almost facing mid-on. The right elbow will be away from the side. From there the arms and wrists will fling the bat outward and downward so that at the moment of impact the wrists are approximately above the right foot and the point of impact of the ball on the bat is appreciably behind it.

The Grip

Having dealt with certain generalities, we now move to the very important topic like the grip. The first requisite of any batsman is to get his grip right, and it is recently observed that an interesting method of attaining it. A splendid coach was asked by a lad what was the correct grip. The coach told the boy to lay his bat face down on the ground with the handle pointing towards him and then to stoop down and pick it up with two hands as though proposing to use it. The boy did and was immediately told that was his proper grip.

Try it out see what result you get. The batsman should not be dogmatic and superstitious about one's grip, because it is believed that various hold can be satisfactory. So much depends on the batsman's methods. Notice that the inverted 'V' formed by the thumb and first finger of the right hand is straight in line with the insertion of the handle down the back of the blade. The bottom hand will be an inch or two from the shoulder of the blade. For the position of my left hand, look at the illustration. This is what might be termed, in golfing parlance, a slightly shut face. It is thought that it will helps the batsman to keep the ball on the ground, especially when playing on-side strokes. However, it is unhesitatingly admit that the left wrist could be more towards the front than mine and be perfectly correct.

The use of wrist and arms and the method of stroke production cannot be stereotyped. There is much to be said in favour of keeping the two hands in the happy medium position of maximum power and control. The left-hand position must remain firm irrespective of the attempted stroke, but the right hand may be allowed to move down the blade for greater control in defensive strokes.

9

BACK LIFT

The back lift is one of the important strokes that a batsman often wish to play while tackling the bowlers. Reams of matter have been written about the necessity of taking one's bat back perfectly straight. Some coaching books even advocate taking the bat back over the stumps.

Too many players fail because their thoughts are concentrated on where their left elbow is or where something else is, instead of hitting the ball. Then it was clear that the initial bat movement almost invariably was towards the slips. This was accentuated by the batsmen's grip and stance and perhaps it should have been straighter, but to me, anyway, the important thing was where the bat went on the down swing. For defensive shots the bat should naturally be as straight as possible, but for back lift would make it far harder to execute the stroke. By going to extremes the player who uses the crease area and takes the bat back absolutely straight would find himself out hit wicket, So long as the batsman is in the correct position at the top of the back lift, the batsman should not go far wrong. If we could take moving pictures of all leading batsman in action, particularly when they were not conscious that a camera was focused on them, it is thought that the cricketers would find the majority of them take the blade back rather more towards first or second slip.

Remember, that the higher the back lift the longer it will take to bring the bat down. There is always a happy medium, but the back lift should be no higher than is necessary for a proper balance between control in defence and power in attack. Some coaches teach players to take the bat some with the left hand. Again there is a little embarrassment about the mental result. A defensive complex starts to build up. Everything in batting leads up to stroke play which may be divided into (a) defensive shots and (b) attacking shots. Again each may be classified into two sections, (a) strokes played with the weight predominantly on the front foot, (b) strokes played with the weight predominantly on the back foot.

10

TAKING GUARD OR BLOCK

Every batsman, upon arriving at the crease, must take block. There are three common positions; middle stump, leg stump, and two legs stump.

It was heard once that a batsman ask for middle and leg inclined to leg, but it is thought that he was stretching things a bat too far. The sole purpose of taking guard is to enable the batsman to judge the direction of the ball relative to his wicket. Spectators sometimes wonder why batsmen may ask for guard several times during an innings. The answer is that a mark on the ground may become obliterated or damaged. Occasionally the two batsmen at the wickets take a different block or one may be a left-hander.

Obviously the one is inclined to make rather a mess of the other fellow's mark, especially if he is the nervous type who is constantly patting the ground whilst awaiting delivery of the ball. The springs can also tear across one's mark when making certain foot movements. It does not always matter and important pertaining the position of the guard. For many batsman's conscience, the middle leg as the most serviceable for taking guard. It means your legs are straightened originally some two inches more towards the leg side than they would be if you look middle stump. In this way it is easier to be sure that a ball travelling towards your pads is outside the leg stumps. And precise judgement of the direction of a ball is a "must" in developing the batting art. When an off-break bowler is operating to a strong leg field, many batsmen take guard on the leg stump or even, in extreme cases, just outside. By so doing they endeavour to counter his wiles. They feel it gives them greater freedom to hit at any ball directed at their pads, and a better chance of steering away from the clutching hands of leg slips any ball directed at the stumps. There is much to be said for the theory.

On the other hand a batsman whose great weakness is that he fails to cover the ball outside the off-stump especially against a fast or medium-pace attack, would be wise to consider taking middle stump for his guard. It would take him those extra couple of inches towards the line of flight before the ball is delivered. So take your choice. You will have to stand or fall by your judgement.

11

DRIVES PLAYED
IN BATTING

OFF DRIVE

It is one of the important drives played in cricket by the batsmen. It is usually being played to the balls comes off the length to the off-side; but not necessarily off line.

Offdrive is a defensive shot played by the batsmen to play a long innings. Its an extension of a defensive shot. If you are in a position early you can play a forcing attacking shot from that position even to a good ball. This is the drive. With the drive, you get into a similar position of a defensive shot , but only this time you extend the bat play. You go through with the swing in the direction of the ball and follow through of the bat is in the direction of the shot.

Offdrive is being played to a ball that is around the off stump. It is being played in the region of mid-off,

COVER DRIVE

It is the most important drives usually played in the extra cover region. It is being played to the ball comes slightly wider to the batsman.

SQUARE DRIVE

The shot which is being played squarer to the wider delivery on the off stump of the batsman is called square drive.

ON DRIVE

The stroke which is being played between mid on and mid wicket is called

A rare shot these days played between mid on and mid wicket.

STRAIGHT DRIVE

It is favourite drives that mostly cricketers used to play. To play straight drive the batsman should get besides the line and pitch of the ball. The batsman should get his head slightly low and top of the ball, thus keeping his body weight forward.

It will also get that power and letting the bat follow through, in the direction of the shot will get you that extra run.

The following are some points to remember while playing the straight drive :

1. The batsman should go for the straight drive on the over pitched delivery which come in the direction of middle, off or on side of the field.

2. The backlift should be high while playing the straight drive.

3. The batsman should stand on the crease in such a way that his head and front shoulder should lead on the line of the ball.

4. The batsman should move his head and shoulder in line and towards the pitch of the ball.

5. The batsman should pay appropriate attention on the position of the head and shoulder towards the line of the ball which is the prime requisite of the short.

6. The batsman should put the front foot forwads and alongside the line of the ball as close as possible.

7. There should be no pivot on the back foot of the batsman.

8. The batsman should adhere to a short stride which enables him to maintain his body balance which is essential for playing any stroke so as the straight drive.

9. The batsman should extend his back leg and grounded on the inside of the toe, thus making the correct weight transfer.

10. The batsman's head should tucked into the shoulder, the batsman should bend his left elbow and the front hip leans towards the ball as a unit.

11. The batsman should perform the full follow through by making good balancing.

12. The batsman should swing down his bat perpendicularly from the top of the backlift with the position that demands his top hand in control and the bottom hand changing in a forefinger/thumb grip.

The batsman should pay particular attention to avoid some common errors and keep the following tips in mind while playing the straight drive :

1. The batsman should not lead with his head and left shoulder instead of he should bring his eyes and body balance on to the line of the ball.

2. The batsman should allow the right hand to come into the stroke too early so that the arc is being shortened and pulled across the line instead of being kept long, flat and smooth, with the bat face travelling down the line for as long as possible.

3. The batsman should not endeavour to hit hard with unbalance body position.

BACK FOOT DRIVE

Usually this drive is not easy to play like front foot drive. To play back foot drive, the batsman should stand tall on the balls of his feet keeping his head level and steady, his front elbow should be pulled skywards allowing the batsman to play the backfoot drive. One that will bring the crowd on their feet.

Back Foot Drive is the most famous batting strokes used in cricket by most of the batsmen. This enables the batsmen to score more runs between the area between the mid-on and cover. The back foot drive is usually played to a delivery just short of a length by good footwork and accurate balancing of body weight.

Unlike the other batting strokes viz., square cut, hook which demands power, strength, the back foot drive needs only right timing and placement.

The following coaching tips will help a batsman/learner to play the back foot drive correctly :

1. The batsman should play back foot drive with the straight bat with full control of the shot.

2. The batsmen's head should be over the ball in order to prevent the ball spooning to cover.

3. The batsman should transfer his body weight forwardly in order to keep the ball on the ground level and to play the stroke more neatly.

4. The batsman should follow through his bat along with the hands in line with the ball, thus he should finish the stroke in a high position.

5. In order to get power to play the back foot drive, the batsman should control the stroke with the top hand with the assistance of bottom hand punching through the ball.

Review of Back Foot Drive Skills

In order to play the back foot drive cleanly, the batsman should follow the following coaching points:

1. The batsman should be a well judge while facing the deliveries from the bowler.

2. The batsman should swing his bat back straight and high to play this stroke.

3. The batsman should move his head along with the shoulder in line and towards the pitch of the balls coming to him.

4. The batsman should slightly lean into the ball with his front shoulder, side elbow and knee.

5. The batsman should transfer his body weight on his front foot with his front toe pointing to mid-off and extra cover of the field.

6. The batsman should pegged his back foot on to the ground with back and across in order to allow appropriate space for playing his stroke.

7. The batsman should step forward with his front foot in line and pitch of the ball.

8. The batsman should be well-balanced all the times he is on the crease and should calmly watch the ball.

9. The batsman should brush his front pad with his bat as he hit the ball.

10. The batsman should keep his body steady with shoulders, arms and bat.

11. The eyes of the batsman should always to the ball.

The batsman should pay particular attention to avoid some common errors and keep the following tips in mind while playing the straight drive :

1. The batsman should not let his top hand to control

the ball.

2. The batsman should not keep his top elbow high enough.

3. The batsman should not keep sideways to the line of the stroke.

4. The batsman should not step far enough back with his back foot and should not move far enough over to get on to the line of the ball.

5. The batsman should not keep the head balance of his body forward while in contact with the delivery.

6. The batsman should not put his hands up so high in the back lift.

12

THE PULL

The shot which is being played to a short ball in length and bouncing adequately is called *The Pull*.

To play the pull shot, the following coaching tips should be followed by the batsman :

1. The batsman should get his rear foot across to the off stump.

2. The batsman should get himself outside the line of the ball.

3. His front foot should swing to the legside in order to open up.

4. The batsman should get outside the line of the ball.

5. The batsman should swing his bat horizontally in front of the body.

6. The batsman should get close his bat in front of his body in order to play the pull shot.

7. The above mentioned tips should be finished with precise follow through with the ball.

It simply consisted of going back and across with the right foot and pulling the ball with a horizontal bat somewhere between mid-on and square-leg.

By the grip, the batsman is able to roll his wrist over to play the stroke and keep the ball on the ground. Keen eyesight is needed, and one have to be careful the ball did not keep low, but this seldom happened on the coir mats.

Actually, there is no other way to play the pull shot than with a cross bat, but on turf greater judgement is required and the stroke must be used more sparingly. A medium-pace bowler quite often operates without a fieldsman between mid-on and square-leg, and this huge unprotected are is most inviting. Even if a man is stationed there, one has plenty of room on either side. Slow bowlers usually have a man or two on the fence, but a pull shot can be played with very great power and it there may still be a reasonable hope of getting four runs. No batsman should attempt to pull a ball which is over-pitched or of good length. This is courting disaster.

However, assuming the ball to be the right shot, the method is very similar to the hook shot. Go back and across with the right foot so that the right toe is pointing almost straight down the pitch towards the bowler. Then as the ball comes along pull it hard to mid-wicket—at the same time pivoting the body and rolling the wrists over to keep the ball on the ground. In many respects the movement is similar to a square cut, but instead of cutting against the line of flight, you pull with it.

In order to control the shot and to have the best chance of combating any uneven bounce, it is essential to pivot the body and to get the legs fairly well apart.

The ball can be struck satisfactory but it will automatically go in the air and the slightest mis-hit will cause it to fly off the top edge of the bat. That is one reason why so few first-class players try the shot at all. For them it isn't worth the risk. But they are missing a grand scoring medium. The stroke is particularly effective against a slow leg-break bowler should he stray in his length. It then becomes a natural, even though it means hitting against the break and thereby flaunting one of cricket's so-called sacred principles. Also it is tremendously valuable against the off-spinner with a

close leg field. There is nothing like a full-blooded pull shot right into the teeth of the short-leg fieldsmen to disturb their confidence and shift them back a yard or two.

That in itself is a big contribution in minimising their danger. If there is no outfield at all the ball can deliberately be lofted over the men close in, but the shot is such a powerful one and it is seldom used, except with full power, that is considered to be the most satisfactory to hit the ball mainly on to the ground and be content with trying to place it between the fieldsmen. At the finish of the shot the batsman will find himself facing square-leg, providing he has pivoted correctly and his swung right through the ball.

In addition to rolling his wrists the striker should, if possible, always keep the blade of the bat not quite horizontal and pointing slightly downwards. This is of further assistance in keeping the ball on the ground. A batsman need not hesitate to pull a ball from outside the off stump. The risk of pulling it on to the stumps from the underside of the bat is negligible, and in any case the legs are positioned so that they would stand a good chance of intercepting such a mis-hit. I advocate concentrated net practice to perfect the technique, and repeat my warning not to try to pull the ball unless it is pitched well short of a length.

The difference between the two pull shots is this. Instead of putting the right foot back and across to the off side, just put the right foot straight back. Then, as the ball is hit between mid-on and square-leg, pull your body away from the line of flight as the left foot is swung round to the leg side whilst you pivot on the right foot. In this way tremendous power can be generated, even more than with the other method, because there seems to be scope for greater leverage. The whole mechanism of the wrists, arms and body can be harnessed to give the ball tremendous crack. Should the ball be missed, it will pass on the off side of the body, often with fatal results, because the ideal ball to pull in this way is one delivered on the stump. With the orthodox pull one has to finish within the crease area and must be careful, in swinging the body round, not to hit the stumps.

But this way there is virtually no limit to the pivotal action which ends with the weight on the left leg. If a fast bowler is trying to engineer a catch on the leg side off a hook shot, this alternative type of pull shot offers a counter because it holds better prospects of pulling a ball which is counting quite high and still keeping it down.

The pull shot is one of the aggressive batting strokes that is being played off the back foot towards the leg side to the ball comes shorter and wider of the off-stumps and to the short-pitched deliveries.

The pull stroke is unlike the hook stroke but seems to be like the hook. It is usually played on or around the waist height.

The following coaching tips will enables a batsman to play the pull shot perfectly:

1. The batsman should play the pull stroke with extended arms in front of the body and usually hit in front of square.

2. The batsman should stand in a correct position with correct timing and good footwork in order to play the desired pull shot.

3. It is another risky shot like that of the Hook, so the batsman should pay appropriate attention while attempting the short-pitched deliveries to the fence otherwise the batsman may get himself hurt or give his wicket cheaply.

4. The batsman should move his back foot back and across as soon as the backswing begins.

5. The batsman should roll his wrists at the correct timing in order to keep the ball played on the ground.

6. The batsman should make the base to play the pull shot by keeping his front leg moved back and towards the leg side.

7. The batsman should keep his head slightly forward and steady all the times he play the pull shot.

8. The batsman should bring down and across his

bat in order to make contact with the ball in front of the body.

9. The batsman should hit the ball downwards by keeping his body weight on the front foot.

10. The batsman should maintain appropriate bodily weight throughout the follow through.

The above mentioned coaching tips will enables the batsman to play the pull stroke more comfortably and safely.

REVIEW OF PULL SHOT SKILLS

The batsman should follow the following coaching tips to play the pull shot :

1. The batsman should endeavour to play the pull shot only to the deliveries which is short pitch in nature and bounces normally and rises between the batsman's waist and shoulders.

2. The line of the ball must be within the reach of the batsman on the off, middle or leg side of the pitch.

3. The batsman should lift his bat before the bowler releases the ball in line with the middle and off stump.

4. The batsman should perform backlift in such a manner that his bat's blades should open and swings back horizontally behind his head.

5. The batsman should always keep his head steady and eyes should be levelled.

6. The batsman should open his shoulder slightly towards the mid-on area.

7. The batsman should move back his head across, inside or outside the line and pitch of the deliveries.

13

SQUARE CUT

It is yet another cricket stroke which is usually used by most of the batsman to play the balls slightly wider in off-side. It is a horizontal bat shot. The following tips should be followed in order to play this stroke :

1. The batsman should be very alert while standing on the crease.

2. He should always keep his eyes on the ball.

3. As soon as the ball comes wider to the off stump, the batsman should get his backfoot close to the stumps in line with the off stump.

4. He should free his arms and get his wrists close to the top of the ball.

5. The face of his bat should be top of the bounce of

the ball.

6. The batsman should always keep his head steady and towards the bowler.

7. The batsman should transfer his body weight on to the back foot.

8. He should keep his head on top of the ball.

9. The batsman should not drop his head back.

10. He should not lose his control of the shot.

11. The batsman should get tall on the ball of his feet and should endeavour to get his eyes on the top of the ball.

12. The batsman should always play the square cut down.

13. Initially, the batsman should slightly back lift his bat, this will assist him to play this stroke more perfectly

14. To play this stroke, the batsman should use his bottom hand and wrist rather than the top hand as this is a bottom hand shot.

There are two squares cuts—the one played off the front foot, the other off the back foot. Let me deal first with the cut off the front foot, which is the more beautiful an powerful but unfortunately seldom seen. With the modern emphasis on back play so many batsmen are always retreating. They are not thinking of, nor are they ready to make, the forward cut even though the ball may warrant it. Also it requires a very bad length ball for one to have the time to judge the shot and really go into with full power. However, assuming the ball is sufficiently short in length, and wide of the off stump, this is one of the most thrilling shots to play.

Obviously, it must be made with a more or less horizontal blade and therefore the margin of error is small. Before the ball lands, no striker can be sure how high it will bounce, but his aim should be to hit the ball near the apex of its fight after bouncing and that will be just in front of the batting crease. The left leg should be advanced forward and across the wicket so that it finishes with the toe directed between point and cover and the left leg carrying the full weight. The left shoulder at the start of the swing should be pointing towards mid-off so that the maximum power can be put into the swing. The shoulders turn only with the impetus of the hit, which is made with the full force of right hand, forearm and shoulder. If anything, the ball should be hit slightly down and the wrists rolled over, shutting the blade of the bat as contact is made.

In this way the ball will be kept on the ground and not cut into the air. Its direction should normally be in front of point and just backward of cover. Cut really hard—don't toy with it. Make the shot a full swing and not a jerk, otherwise it may tend to shift your head position and divert the eyes from the ball. As I suggested previously the square cut off the back foot is much more prevalent than the forward square cut. Understandably so, because first it can be played off a ball which is not so deficient in length, and secondly because the natural tendency of batsmen is to take the easy road and give themselves the maximum amount of time in which to see the ball and make the stroke. The direction of the ball is the same in both cases. So long as it is short enough and well clear of the off stump, the batsman composition himself to make a cut either just behind point or even past the gully position. The same essential must be applied as off the front foot. Hit slightly down on the ball as the weight is transferred to the right leg. Flex the knee slightly to assist balance. Hit firmly and freely but not jerkily. This stroke does not command the same power as the other one. More care should be taken to see that no mistake is made and that it is carefully placed.

One on the top edge will often fly over slips and one on the bottom edge seldom causes any harm. The ideal height for cutting is a ball slightly over stump high, but naturally one has to hit the ball wherever, it is. Bounce cannot be regulated by the batsman. With the end of the blade slightly lower than the handle as the ball is struck, and the turn of the wrists, it is not difficult to cut the ball downwards, thereby eliminating the risk of a catch to point.

Footwork

How often have we heard the saying "Adam Gilchrist is a great batsman—his footwork is superb." What is meant by this term footwork? It is not a question which can be answered simply, even though instinctively a cricketer knows what is meant. Obviously, good footwork implies correct footwork. Perhaps it does. But what is the use of a man going back on to his stumps in the approved fashion if he moves so slowly that he is late in completing his shot and is trapped LBW. This surely means one requires speed as well. But too much speed may bring disaster.

If one jumps out to drive, gets there too soon and lofts a catch, that could be fatal. Conversely, it is oftenly seen a player jump out to drive only to drive only to find himself too short, yet by speed footwork regain his crease in time to prevent a stumping. Therefore, speed can at times overcome faulty judgement. These reflections cause me to say that basically, to be good, footwork should be correct, it should be of the required speed and it must be co-ordinated with perfect judgement.

Certainly it should it never be too slow. One of the outstanding characteristics of great players is the apparent ease with which they play their shots. They always seem to be in the right position with plenty of time to spare. There may have been some who were nearly great—men who relied upon forward play and whose scores were mainly compiled by driving—but it is observed in terms of batsmen who were able to command every shot in the book and were at home to all classes of bowling. In doubt if one could truthfully say there is any single key to batsmanship, but footwork is certainly one of the keys to unlock the innermost secrets.

Down the Gully

Sometimes opportunities provide themselves of picking up singles down the gully to third-man. When a fast or medium-pace bowler drops the ball a little short outside the off stump, it is quite simple to make a position similar to that for the square cut off the right foot, only this time, instead of cutting with power, get more on top of and closer to the ball, hit slightly later, and glide it wide of third slip.

The pace of the ball itself will produce the desired result without any real assistance from the batsman. It is not dangerous providing the striker is well over the ball and makes sure of hitting it down on to the ground. This is particularly necessary if a fieldsman is stationed at third slip or at backward point. The main danger lies in a ball which unexpectedly lifts off the pitch. That is why it is necessary to be well across and on top of the line of flight.

CONCLUSION

Usually square cut is played on the ball comes a short and slightly wide outside the off-stump. It is most favourite stroke played by many left-handed batsmen.

Square cut is easily played by the left-handed batsmen because left-handers are free to turn the delivery which comes to them slightly slanted.

To play square cut perfectly, the batsmen should follow the following coaching tips :

1. In order to play square cut most prominently, the batsman should free his arms and should hit the ball with the crossed bat with plenty of power.

2. The batsman should roll his wrists by keeping his body weight on the top of the ball. Thus, the batsman play square cut safely.

3. The batsman should move his back foot back towards the stumps and across towards the line of the delivery.

4. The batsman should bring his bat down and across with full arm extension in order to play the square cut.

5. As the bat is taken back, the front shoulder of the batsman should be turned to the offside.

6. In order to keep the ball down, the batsman should keep his head still and should roll his wrists forwards. This will make a batsman comfortable to play his desired stroke.

7. The batsman should place his body weight on the back foot. By doing this, he should finish the stroke by the bat finishing over the front shoulder and behind the head.

All the above mentioned coaching tips will definitely help and guide a batsman, learner to play the square cut perfectly.

Review of Square Cut Skills

In order to play square cut cleanly, the batsmen should follow the following coaching tips :

1. The batsman should always endeavour to play

square cut safely to the balls which is wide of the off stump and that is about waist height.

2. The batsman should always be controlled of his stroke.

3. The batsman should lift his bat back straight as soon as the bowler is began to run-up for bowling.

4. The batsman should pull his bat with his bottom hand behind his rear shoulder and horizontally behind his head.

5. The batsman should watch the ball along the line of the front shoulder.

6. The eyes of the batsman should be fixed on the point of contact with the ball.

7. The batsman should keep his head still, particularly at impact.

8. The batsman should move his head and eyes as he transfer his body weight to a position above his back bent knee.

9. The eyes of the batsman should never be able to get right behind the flight.

10. The toes of the back foot should point towards the point region.

11. The batsman should move his foot back and across the wickets towards the off-side region of the field.

12. The batsman should always put his body weight on the back foot leaving his front foot resting on the on the ground.

13. The batsman should draw slightly his front foot towards the back foot.

14. The batsman should lift his front foot on follow through with his toes providing the appropriate balance.

15. The batsman should always keep his bodily weight on his back foot.

16. The batsman should bring his bat down and across the front of his body at arms length just finishing over the front shoulder.

17. The batsman should straighten his arms and strike at the ball downwards at a point level with the his back hip.

18. The batsman should always swing his bat horizontally from behind the back shoulder.

The batsman should pay particular attention to avoid some common errors and keep the following tips in mind while playing the square cut :

1. The batsman should hit the ball high on the bat.

2. The batsman should not get his bat up so high in order to ensure it coming down on to the ball from above.

3. The batsman should not cut the ball so hardly in order to avoid the errors.

4. The batsman should not make haste in playing the square cut to the wide shot-pitched deliveries rather he should strike the ball with steadily with popping crease.

14

LEG GLANCE

The leg glance is a stroke made forcefully with the wrists and forearms, the ball usually travels between the square-leg and fine-leg. There are two types of glance strokes. One is off the front foot and the other by moving back to the wickets.

Leg Glance Off the Front Foot

This stroke is played most effectively to the ball pitched between the good length and half-volley, just outside the batsman's left leg. It is played off fast, medium or off-spin balls.

Do not attempt it off a leg-spinner as there are chances of the ball touching the outer edge of the bat with a resultant catch in the slips. And also do not attempt on any type of bowling if leg slips are there. Take the left foot up the wicket so that it is inside the line of flight. The bat comes down over the off-stump toward mid-on. At the moment of contact, push the left hand well forward and allow the body to lean over the front leg. The angle of deflection will depend on the extent to which the bat face is shut at the moment of impact.

Leg Glance Off the Back Foot

This stroke is made to the ball pitched just short of length, on or just outside, the batsman's left leg. The right foot is taken back towards the middle stump with its toe pointing to cover-point. The left foot is taken near the right leg and it should point towards mid-off. This

brings the trunk of the body sufficiently round to enable the batsman to see the ball clearly.

The following coaching tips will help the batsman to play the leg glance perfectly and in a right manner:

1. The batsman should move both feet back towards the stumps by opening the body out towards the ball.
2. The leg stump of the batsman should always be covered while playing leg glance.
3. The batsman should keep his head forward in line with the ball and in order to face the delivery.
4. The batsman should bring his bat as straight a line as possible.
5. The batsman should turn the bat face towards the leg side and should make effort in order to contact with the ball in front of the body.
6. The batsman should control the shot with his top hand in order to glance away the ball.

15

BATTING RULES

BASICS

Cricket is a team sport for two teams of eleven players each. A formal game of cricket can last anything from an afternoon to several days.

Although the game play and rules are very different, the basic concept of cricket is similar to that of baseball. Teams bat in successive innings and attempt to score runs, while the opposing team fields and attempts to bring an end to the batting team's innings. After each team has batted an equal number of innings, depending on conditions chosen before the game, the team with the most runs wins.

EQUIPMENTS

Protective Gear

The batsman usually accompanied with the protective gears viz., pads, gloves, helmet, etc., to avoid any injuries occurred while facing fast bowlers.

Cricket Bat

Cricket bat is made up of high quality of woods. Bat's blade made of willow, flat on one side, humped on the other for strength, attached to a sturdy cane handle. The blade has a maximum width of 108 millimetres (4.25 inches) and the whole bat has a maximum length of 965 millimetres (38 inches).

Clothing

The batsman usually wear long trousers, shirt which is white in colour and which may be long-sleeved woollen pullover in cold weather or half-sleeved in summer.

Commonly, the colour of the clothing of the players are white in colour with the red ball. While playing with a white ball, the colour of the clothing of the players should be in solid team colours. To avoid sun screening and rays, the players usually wear hat or cap.

Shoes

The batsman usually wear leather shoes with the soles that have adequate and firm grip while walking on the grass-ground.

THE FIELD

A cricket field is a roughly elliptical field of flat grass, ranging in size from about 90 to 150 metres (100-160 yards) across, bounded by an obvious fence or other marker. There is no fixed size or shape for the field, although large deviations from a low-eccentricity ellipse are discouraged.

In the centre of the field, and usually aligned along the long axis of the ellipse, is the pitch, a carefully prepared rectangle of closely mown and rolled grass over hard packed earth. It is marked with white lines, called creases, like this:

The dimensions are in centimetres (divide by 2.54 for inches).

BATSMAN'S SHOTS

The different types of shots a batsman can play are described by names:

Drive

An offensive shot played with the bat sweeping down through the vertical. The ball travels swiftly along the ground in front of the striker. A drive can be an on drive, straight drive, off drive, or cover drive, depending in which direction it goes.

Reverse Sweep
A sweep with the bat reversed, into the point area.

Block
A defensive shot played with the bat vertical and angled down at the front, intended to stop the ball and drop it down quickly on to the pitch in front of the batsman.

Cut
A shot played with the bat close to horizontal, which hits the ball somewhere in the arc between cover and gully.

Edge, or Glance
A shot played off the bat at a glancing angle, through the slips area.

Pull
A horizontal bat shot which pulls the ball around the batsman into the square leg area.

Leg Glance
A shot played at a glancing angle behind the legs, so that it goes in the direction of fine leg.

Sweep
Like a pull shot, except played with the backmost knee on the ground, so as to hit balls which bounce low.

French Cut
An attempt at a cut shot which hits the bottom edge of the bat and goes into the area behind square leg.

Hook
Like a pull shot, but played to a bouncer and intended to hit the ball high in the air over square leg - hopefully for six runs.

Most of these shots can also be lofted, in an attempt to hit the ball over the close fielders (or the boundary). The batting strokes can be divided into two categories: Straight bat and cross bat. The straight bat shots are played with the bat held close to the vertical, and are the blocks, drives and glances. Cross bat shots are played with the bat held more horizontally, like a baseball bat. These include cuts, pulls, sweeps and hooks.

SCORING RUNS

To get the runs, the batsman has to hit the ball to the gap between the fielders in the field. The batsman usually earn the runs by hitting the ball to the gap and then running between the popping creases. When they both reach the opposite crease, one run is scored, and they may return for another run immediately.

The fielding side attempts to prevent runs being scored by threatening to run out one of the batsmen. If the batsmen are endeavouring to take runs, and a fielder gathers the ball and hits a wicket with it, dislodging one or both bails, while no batsman is behind that wicket's popping crease, then the nearest batsman is run out.

Usually, the batsmen carry their bats as they run, and turning for another run is accomplished by touching the ground beyond the crease with an outstretched bat. The batsmen do not have to run at any time they think it is unsafe - it is common to hit the ball and elect not to run.

In addition to scoring runs like this, if a batsman hits the ball so that it reaches the boundary fence, he scores four runs, without needing to actually run them. If a batsman hits the ball over the boundary on the full, he scores six runs. If a four or six is scored, the ball is completed and the batsmen cannot be run out. If a spectator encroaches on to the field and touches the ball, it is considered to have reached the boundary. If a fielder gathers the ball, but then steps outside or touches the boundary while still holding the ball, four runs are scored. If a fielder catches the ball on the full and, either during or immediately after the catch, steps outside or touches the boundary, six runs are scored.

Runs scored by a batsman, including all overthrows, are credited to him by the scorer. The number of runs, scored by each batsman is an important statistic and will add into his individual total and record summary.

EXTRAS RUNS

Extra runs means the runs made by other means such as : leg bye, bye, over throw, no-ball, wide-ball etc., other than from the batsman's score.

The total number of runs for the innings is equal to the sums of the individual batsmen's scores and the extras. The extra runs are treated separately and recorded separately at the team's total.

OFFICIALS

The game of cricket is administered by the two umpires who take all the decisions and their decision have to be followed by the players on the field.

One umpire is standing opposite the batsman and close the bowler's run-up zone; he is responsible for taking The other umpire is taking his position at the leg side (but not always); he is responsible for crucial decisions of run-out, stumpings etc., at his end. The two umpires have to stand on their relative positions and change over their ends and role after the interval of each over bowled by the bowler.

In the modern cricket, there is the availability of the technology and provision for the third umpire which usually sit off the field with a television replay monitor. At his presence in the game of cricket, the two field umpires usually go for his decision when they are unsure of their decision in a complicated situations; the field umpires exhibit the appropriate signal to seek the decision of the third umpire usually in the critical situation of run-out, stumpings, catching etc.

NIGHTWATCHMAN

A batsman which is sent to bat out of order towards the end of a day's play in test cricket match to protect the better player is called the *nightwatchman*.